**Date: 10/27/21**

**BR 796.3578 DOW**
**Downs, Kieran,**
**Softball /**

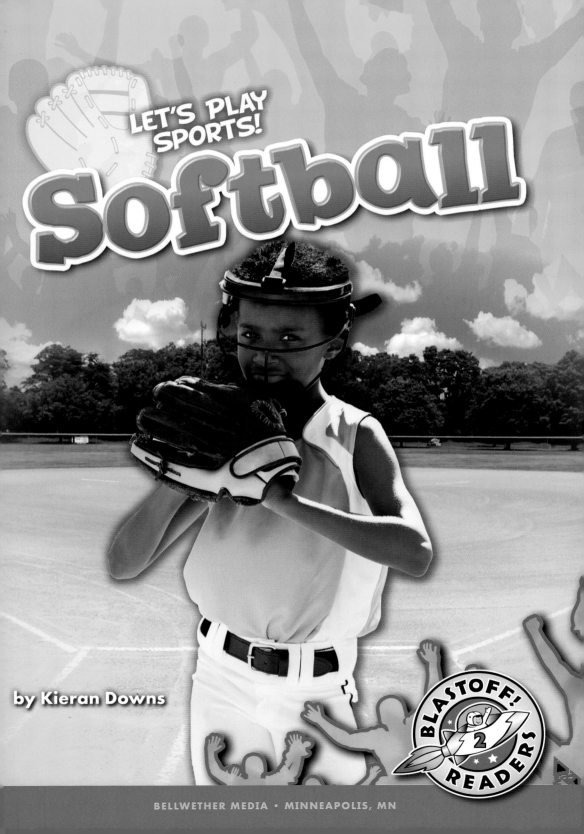

LET'S PLAY SPORTS!

# Softball

by Kieran Downs

BELLWETHER MEDIA • MINNEAPOLIS, MN

BLASTOFF!
2
READERS

**Blastoff! Readers** are carefully developed by literacy experts to build reading stamina and move students toward fluency by combining standards-based content with developmentally appropriate text.

**Level 1** provides the most support through repetition of high-frequency words, light text, predictable sentence patterns, and strong visual support.

**Level 2** offers early readers a bit more challenge through varied sentences, increased text load, and text-supportive special features.

**Level 3** advances early-fluent readers toward fluency through increased text load, less reliance on photos, advancing concepts, longer sentences, and more complex special features.

★ **Blastoff! Universe**

Reading Level

Grade **K** → Grades **1-3** → Grade **4**

This edition first published in 2021 by Bellwether Media, Inc.

No part of this publication may be reproduced in whole or in part without written permission of the publisher. For information regarding permission, write to Bellwether Media, Inc., Attention: Permissions Department, 6012 Blue Circle Drive, Minnetonka, MN 55343.

Library of Congress Cataloging-in-Publication Data

Names: Downs, Kieran, author.
Title: Softball / by Kieran Downs.
Description: Minneapolis, MN : Bellwether Media Inc., 2021. | Series: Blastoff! readers. Let's play sports! | Includes bibliographical references and index. | Audience: Ages 5-8 | Audience: Grades K-1 | Summary: "Relevant images match informative text in this introduction to softball. Intended for students in kindergarten through third grade"– Provided by publisher.
Identifiers: LCCN 2020029201 (print) | LCCN 2020029202 (ebook) | ISBN 9781644874271 (library binding) | ISBN 9781648341045 (ebook)
Subjects: LCSH: Softball–Juvenile literature.
Classification: LCC GV881.15 .D68 2021  (print) | LCC GV881.15  (ebook) | DDC 796.357/8–dc23
LC record available at https://lccn.loc.gov/2020029201
LC ebook record available at https://lccn.loc.gov/2020029202

# Table of Contents

# What Is Softball?

Softball is a sport played between two teams on a field.

Teams try to score **runs**. The team that scores more runs wins the game!

scoring a run

Softball is played around the world. It is one of the most popular sports in the United States.

# CAT OSTERMAN

- Pitcher
- United States Women's National Softball Team
- Accomplishments:
  - USA Softball National Player of the Year 3 times
  - All-American 4 times
  - Team gold medal winner at the 2004 Athens Olympics
  - Team silver medal winner at the 2008 Beijing Olympics

People of all ages play the sport!

# What Are the Rules for Softball?

A softball game lasts seven **innings**. Both teams get a turn at bat during each inning.

The visiting team goes first. The inning ends after both teams get three **outs**.

tagging the batter out

The **pitcher** throws an **underhand** pitch for the batter to hit.

If the batter swings and misses, they get a **strike**. After three strikes, the batter is out.

strike

pitcher

underhand pitch

11

If the batter hits the ball, they run to first base. Anyone already on base runs to the next base.

They score runs when they touch all four bases. Sometimes batters hit a **home run**!

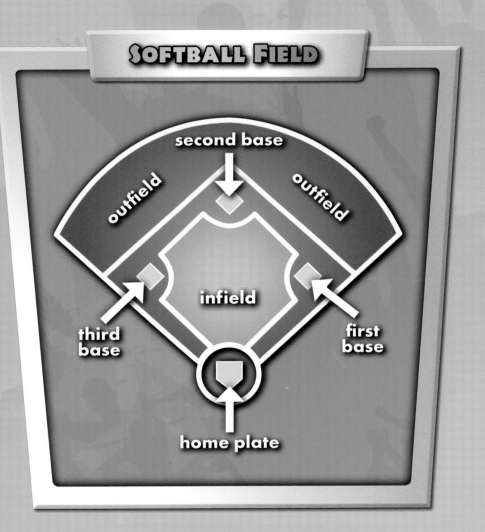

SOFTBALL FIELD

second base

outfield

outfield

infield

third base

first base

home plate

The **defense** tries to get the batter out.

**Fielders** often catch **fly balls**. Catching the ball before it hits the ground is an out.

defense

fly ball

fielder

Fielders also grab **ground balls**. They throw the ball to a base.

ground ball

If the ball beats the batter, the batter is out. Fielders can also tag the batter out.

# Softball Gear

glove

Fielders use gloves to catch the ball.

Players wear shoes with **cleats** to help them run faster.

SOFTBALL GEAR

metal bat

helmet

cleats

glove

19

Batters wear helmets to keep their heads safe.

They use metal bats to hit the ball. Batter up!

helmet

metal
bat

# Glossary

**cleats**—bumps or spikes on the bottom of some shoes to help players run on the field

**defense**—the team that does not have the ball and is trying to keep the other team from scoring

**fielders**—players who play in the infield or outfield

**fly balls**—softballs hit high in the air

**ground balls**—softballs that bounce or roll on the ground after they are hit

**home run**—a hit where the batter runs all the way around the bases and scores a run; home runs are usually hit over the outfield fence.

**innings**—the parts of a softball game in which each team gets a turn at bat

**outs**—when a batter is either tagged by the ball or the ball beats the batter to a base; a batter is also out if they get three strikes at bat.

**pitcher**—the player who throws the ball for the batter to hit

**runs**—points scored by touching home plate after touching the other three bases

**strike**—a ball thrown over home plate between the batter's chest and knees; a strike is also any pitch that is swung at and missed.

**underhand**—referring to a throw made with the arm below shoulder level

# To Learn More

## AT THE LIBRARY

Adamson, Thomas K. *Baseball*. Minneapolis, Minn.: Bellwether Media, 2020.

Meister, Cari. *Softball*. Minneapolis, Minn.: Jump!, 2017.

Streza, Nancy. *My Favorite Sport: Baseball*. Irvine, Calif.: Xist Publishing, 2018.

## ON THE WEB

# FACTSURFER

Factsurfer.com gives you a safe, fun way to find more information.

1. Go to www.factsurfer.com.

2. Enter "softball" into the search box and click 🔍.

3. Select your book cover to see a list of related content.

# Index

The images in this book are reproduced through the courtesy of: kali9, front cover (hero); RogueTeacher, front cover (background); Susan Leggett, pp. 4, 4-5, 20; Susan Leggett/ Alamy, pp. 6, 8; Charles REx Arbogast/ AP Images, p. 7; Frank Paul/ Alamy, p. 9; miws16, p. 10; Zuma Press/ Alamy, pp. 10-11; Khairil Ajhar Jaafar, p. 12; Bruce Leighty-Sports Images/ Alamy, pp. 14, 18; Jamie Roach, p. 15; Cap Sport Media/ Alamy, pp. 16, 20-21; McClatchy-Tribune/ Alamy, p. 17; sirtravelalot, p. 19 (top left); YinYang, p. 19 (top right); Sportlibrary, p. 19 (bottom left); Elena Yakusheva, p. 19 (bottom right); kayannl, p. 23.